Ten Keys to

Happiness

GW00536301

Ten Keys to

Happiness

GUDRUN KRETSCHMANN

Thorsons
An Imprint of HarperCollinsPublishers

Thorsons
An Imprint of HarperCollins *Publishers*
77-85 Fulham Palace Road,
Hammersmith, London W6 8JB

First published in Australia by Angus&Robertson,
25 Ryde Road, Pymble, Sydney, NSW 2073, 1994
Thorsons edition 1994
1 3 5 7 9 10 8 6 4 2

© Gudrun Kretschmann 1994*
Illustrations by Kate Mitchell

Gudrun Kretschmann asserts the moral right to
be identified as the author of this work

A catalogue record for this book
is available from the British Library

ISBN 0 7225 3001 3

Printed in Hong Kong

All rights reserved. No part of this publication may be reproduced,
stored in a retrieval system, or transmitted, in any form or by any
means, electronic, mechanical, photocopying, recording or
otherwise, without the prior permission of the publishers.

Dear Friends

If you apply these 10 keys in your daily
life, happiness is yours, and nobody and
nothing can take it away again.
Happiness starts within, not without.
Here are the keys to enter the kingdom
of inner peace. All you need to do is open
the door.

Peace, Love and Joy

Gudrun

Contents

Choice

I now choose to be happy

You can choose to see the world any way you want. You can choose your thoughts which create actions and reactions (emotions). Your choice of thoughts has formed your life as it is now. Your attitude determines how you experience the world. If you want to change your life, change your thoughts. You can choose a life of peace, joy and happiness. You can decide to stop being affected by the outer world and, instead, to affect the world around you with your peace.

2

Love

I love and approve of myself

Love is the most important ingredient in life. When there is love there is no fear or doubt. It is compassion, forgiveness and total detachment. Love is the ever-extending and expanding life itself. Have faith in love. It is the solution to whatever confronts you, the answer to every question, the healer of every wound, the friend when you feel lonely, the nurturer in hard times. Love cannot be given to you. It can only come from yourself. You do not know that there is love until you have and give it yourself. When you have love for yourself you will see love in everyone and everything, without comparison and judgment.

3

Truth

I now listen to my inner voice of wisdom

*I*f you are indecisive, the way of truth is always the perfect path leading to peace and joy, not confusion. Pay attention with your heart, listen to the unspoken words, for all of these are ways to your inner truth. Truth is healing and it frees you from guilt and anger. Truth is an agent of love wanting to be expressed and followed. Spoken from your heart, it cannot cause conflict or hurt others. On the contrary, it will solve problems and affect the way people look at themselves. Find out what is true for yourself; it may not always be what is true for others. Make truth your daily guide and you will not go astray.

4

Forgiveness

I will not judge today

*H*appiness can be reached only when you practise forgiveness. By forgiving yourself and others you let go of fear, judgment and misery. Forgiveness frees you and allows you to see the good in everyone including yourself. It enables you to correct any perceptions which are not reflecting love. It is not up to you to change anybody, but to accept others as they are. Choose to see innocence in everyone, including yourself. When you have the need to talk about someone else, you have not forgiven. When you have the need to argue, you have not forgiven. When you have the need to justify, you have not forgiven. When you have the need to blame, you have not forgiven.

5

Joy

I am living in the ever-joyous now

person who chooses to see things in a brighter way is usually a much happier person. Your way of looking at situations, people and yourself creates a feeling. Start to see things from the positive side. Joy is a choice. Be positive. If you don't feel like it, act as if you were. Move your body. Step out of the situation that has dragged you down or the thoughts that have made you miserable. Moving your body will move your state of being. Let go of fear and guilt and stay in the present moment, by seeing, smelling, feeling and tasting your surroundings.

6

Balance

I now create peace and harmony in my life

A balance in what you eat, how you feel, what you do, and what you think, is desirable in every aspect of life, as it creates more harmony within yourself and with others. Nature works on the basis of balance. It works in total perfection, where each action is harmonised with another. We are all part of it and function on the same principles. Our society is based on imbalanced motives, such as trying to heal one deficiency with one remedy instead of looking at it as a whole. Attachments and addictions are effects caused by imbalanced thoughts and actions. Let the law of nature control your life.

7

Expression

I now am free to be me

To express yourself is to give yourself the freedom to be you. Denial is the opposite meaning: you do not accept the way you are nor how you feel. Many limitations and restrictions and beliefs have been put on us by society, family, tradition and religion, resulting in guilt. Overcome them, and see what is right for you. Avoid misunderstandings and problems by letting others know what is going on within you — fast — without attacking the other person. Taking it personally is the other person's choice and not your responsibility. Allow yourself to be who you really are and remember that it is none of your business what others think of you.

8

Trust

I now trust that all is well

'Don't worry, be happy!' This statement really needs no further explanation. The past is over, there is nothing you can do about it. And worrying about what might happen in the future does not get you very far either. Let go of the past and future worries. You are not the victim of the world you see, but of your own thoughts. Let go of control and trust that there is a higher intelligence working in perfect order. Allow it to be. By believing and trusting that all is well in your world, you create peace and harmony. Only doubt and fear will stop you from being happy.

9

Gratitude

All that I give is given to myself

Happy people are the ones who are grateful for what they have and what they are. Miserable and depressed people don't know how to say thank you. The more you have, the more grateful you can be. Start off by saying thank you to yourself, appreciate how far you have come and what you have achieved. It could be a lot worse. Giving thanks and appreciation opens many doors. Be grateful even for mistakes and conflicts, because these give you the opportunity to learn and grow. Give and you receive. Remember last time you gave something with love? Was it not really receiving?!

10

Courage

In change is where I grow

Take risks, do something different, come out of your comfort zone. You won't grow personally and spiritually if you are sticking to what you are comfortable with. There might be something great awaiting you on the other side of the lake. Don't let routines and fixed beliefs control your life. Life is ever-changing. There is only one consistency and that is change. It brings aliveness and excitement, growth and fulfilment. You need courage to change and to choose happiness. Then the path to finding happiness can be as exciting as happiness itself.